VENUS

EARLY BIRD
ASTRONOMY

BY PAUL FLEISHER

D1224105

LERNER PUBLICATIONS COMPANY • MINNEAPOLIS

The images in this book are used with the permission of: NASA/JPL, pp. 4, 10, 15, 16, 30, 32, 33, 34, 36 (bottom), 40 (bottom), 41, 46, 47, 48 (both); © MPI/Stringer/Getty Images, pp. 5, 40 (top); © Yoshinori Watabe/amana images/Getty Images, p. 6; © Mike Hewitt/Getty Images, p. 7; © The Bridgeman Art Library/Getty Images, p. 8; © HIP/Art Resource, NY, p. 9; © UPPA/Photoshot, p. 11; © Laura Westlund/Independent Picture Service, pp. 12–13, 18, 19, 37; The International Astronomical Union/Martin Kornmesser, p. 14; ESA, pp. 17, 42; © Attila Kisbenedek/AFP/Getty Images, p. 20; © Jamie Cooper/SSPL/The Image Works, pp. 21, 27 (top); © Dendron/Dreamstime.com, p. 22; © Science Source/Photo Researchers, Inc., pp. 23, 31; © Todd Strand/Independent Picture Service, p. 24; © Ron Miller, pp. 25, 35; © akg-images/RIA Nowosti, p. 26; ESA/CNR-IASF, Rome, Italy and Observatoire de Paris, France, p. 27 (bottom); © SuperStock, p. 28; © Novosti/Photo Researchers, Inc., p. 29; © NASA JPL/Time Life Pictures/Getty Images, p. 36 (top); © Sovfoto, pp. 38, 39; Courtesy of Akihiro Ikeshita/Japan Aerospace Exploration Agency, p. 43.

Front cover: NASA/JPL.
Back cover: NASA, ESA, and the Hubble Heritage Team (STScI/AURA).

Lerner Publications Company
A division of Lerner Publishing Group, Inc.
241 First Avenue North
Minneapolis, MN 55401 U.S.A.

Website address: www.lernerbooks.com

Library of Congress Cataloging-in-Publication Data

Fleisher, Paul.
    Venus / by Paul Fleisher.
        p.   cm. — (Early bird astronomy)
    Includes index.
    ISBN 978–0–7613–4151–2 (lib. bdg. : alk. paper)
    1. Venus (Planet)—Juvenile literature. 2. Solar system—Juvenile literature. I. Title.
QB621.F64 2010
523.42—dc22   2008050762

Manufactured in the United States of America
1 2 3 4 5 6 – BP – 15 14 13 12 11 10

CONTENTS

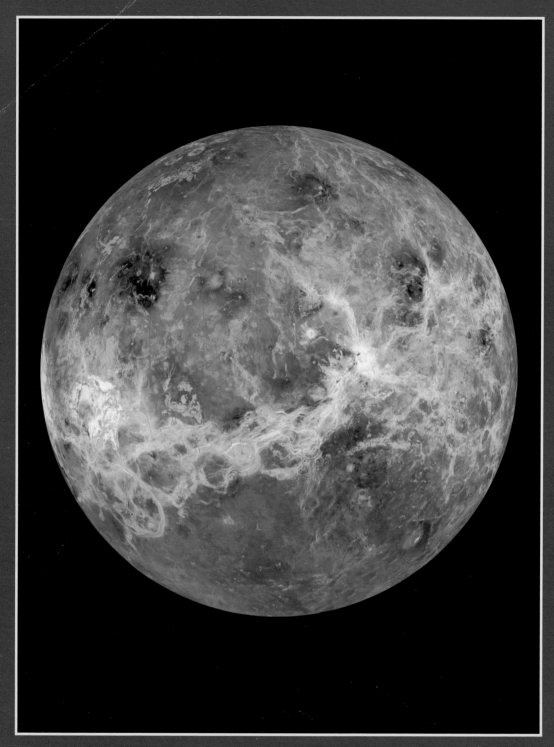

BE A WORD DETECTIVE

Can you find these words as you read about the planet Venus? Be a detective and try to figure out what they mean. You can turn to the glossary on page 46 for help.

asteroid	coronas	solar system
astronomer	day	spacecraft
atmosphere	gravity	telescope
axis	orbit	volcanoes
carbon dioxide	rotate	year

Venus shines brightly in the night sky. Is Venus a star?

CHAPTER 1

FIRST STAR I SEE TONIGHT

No one discovered the planet Venus. No one had to. Venus is the third-brightest thing in the sky. Only the Sun and the Moon are brighter.

People have watched Venus for thousands of years. It's on the first sky chart. That chart was made about 5,000 years ago.

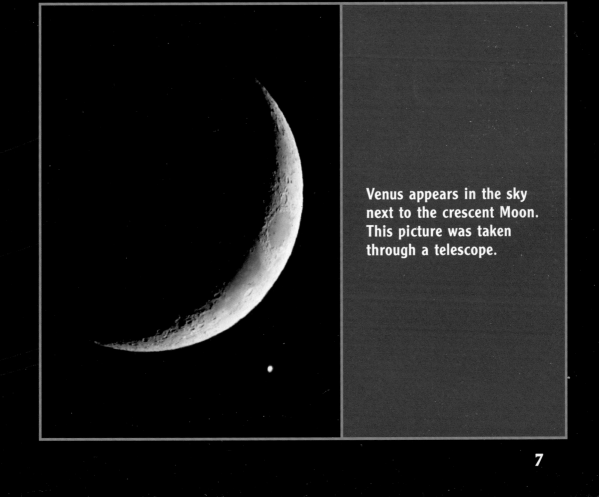

Venus appears in the sky next to the crescent Moon. This picture was taken through a telescope.

Many ancient peoples believed in gods and goddesses. They often named the planets after them. The Persians called the planet Anahita. In the Middle East, it was Ishtar. The Romans called the planet Venus.

Venus was the Roman goddess of love and beauty. The Greeks called her Aphrodite. A Greek artist made this statue called *Venus de Milo* around 130 B.C.

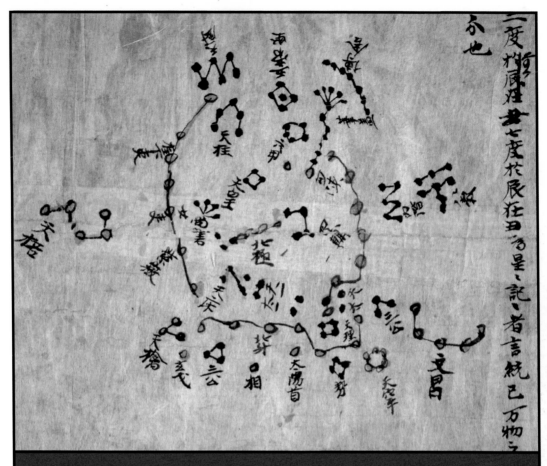

This Chinese star chart was made sometime between A.D. 618 and 906. It uses the position of the planet Jupiter as a guide to studying the stars.

In ancient China, people thought the planet was two different beings. The evening star was Tai-po. The morning star was Nu Chien. They were husband and wife.

9

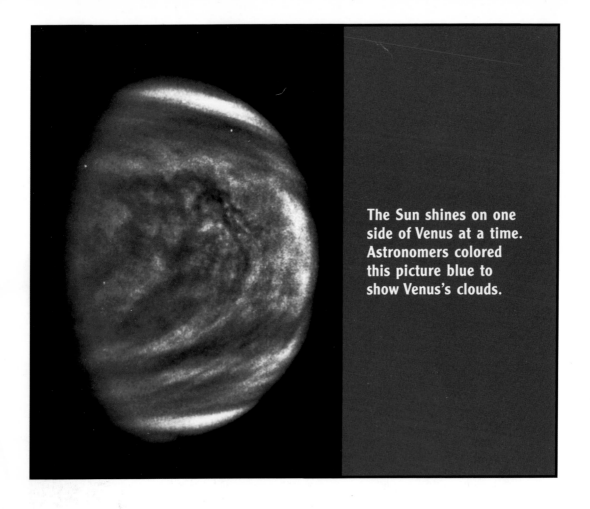

The Sun shines on one side of Venus at a time. Astronomers colored this picture blue to show Venus's clouds.

Stars make their own light. But planets don't. They reflect light from a star called the Sun. Sunlight shines on Venus. It lights the planet.

Venus is near the Sun. It gets a lot of sunlight. Clouds around Venus reflect the light. That's why Venus is so bright.

Venus can fool people. Sometimes people think it's a plane. They may even think it's a spaceship. That's how bright Venus is.

An astronomer explains that a 1966 picture shows Venus and the Moon shining together. Others had claimed that the photo showed a spaceship.

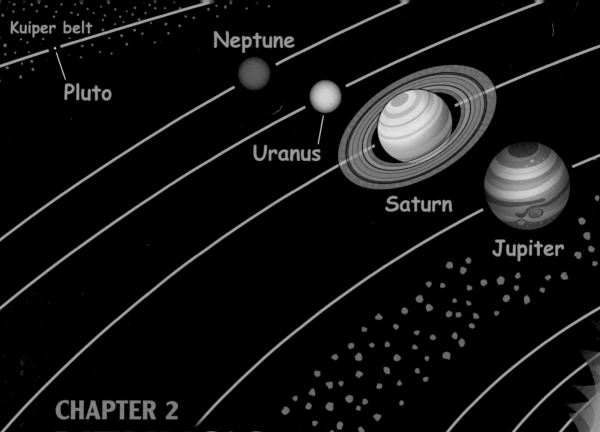

Kuiper belt

Pluto

Neptune

Uranus

Saturn

Jupiter

CHAPTER 2
VENUS'S NEIGHBORHOOD

Venus is part of the solar system. The solar system includes the Sun and eight planets. There are also dwarf planets. They are smaller than the planets. Comets and rocky objects called asteroids (A-stur-oydz) are also part of the solar system.

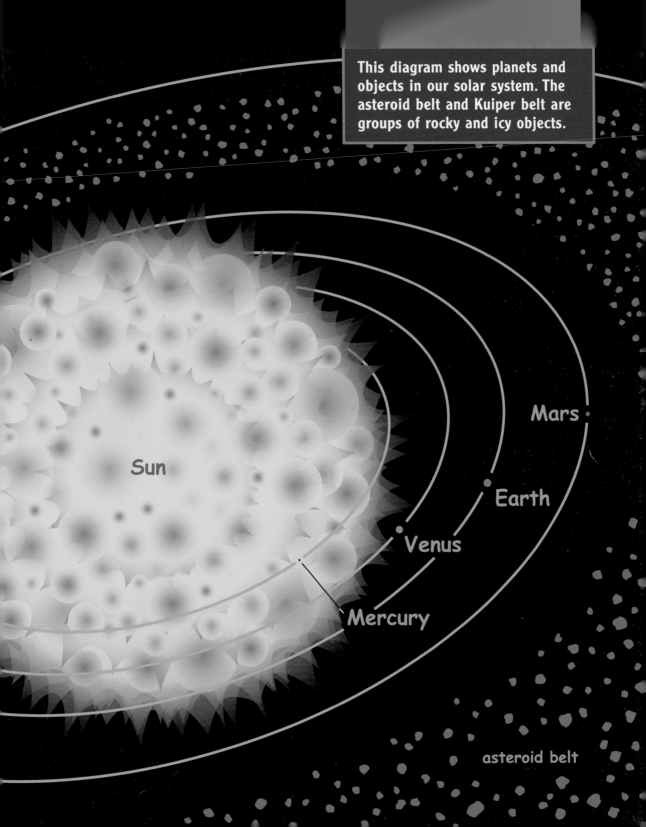

This diagram shows planets and objects in our solar system. The asteroid belt and Kuiper belt are groups of rocky and icy objects.

Mars

Sun

Earth

Venus

Mercury

asteroid belt

This picture shows the Sun (LEFT), the eight planets of our solar system, and the dwarf planet Pluto. In reality, the planets are much farther away from each other.

The Sun is the center of the solar system. Mercury, Venus, Earth, and Mars are the closest planets to the Sun. They are mostly made of solid rock. Scientists call them the rocky planets.

Jupiter, Saturn, Uranus, and Neptune are mostly made of gas. They are called gas giants. They are much larger than the rocky planets.

Between the rocky planets and the gas giants are millions of asteroids. This area is called the asteroid belt.

Six of the planets have moons that circle them. Earth has one moon. The gas giants have many. But Venus has no moons.

The gas giant Saturn (CENTER) has dozens of moons.

Venus (LEFT) is almost the same size as Earth (RIGHT). Like Earth, it has clouds and storms.

Venus is sometimes called Earth's twin. The two planets are almost the same size. Venus is 7,521 miles (12,104 kilometers) across. Earth is 7,926 miles (12,756 km) across. Venus is Earth's closest neighbor. But Venus is very different from Earth.

Venus is a harsh place. It is the hottest planet. It is about 67 million miles (108 million km) from the Sun. Mercury is closer to the Sun. But Venus is hotter. The temperature on Venus is about 864°F (462°C).

An artist created this view of Venus's hot surface.

Planets are always moving. All planets rotate (ROH-tayt). That means they spin like a top. A planet rotates on its axis (AK-sihs). An axis is an imaginary line. It goes through the center of the planet.

A day is the time a planet takes to rotate once. Venus rotates very slowly. It takes 243 Earth days to rotate once.

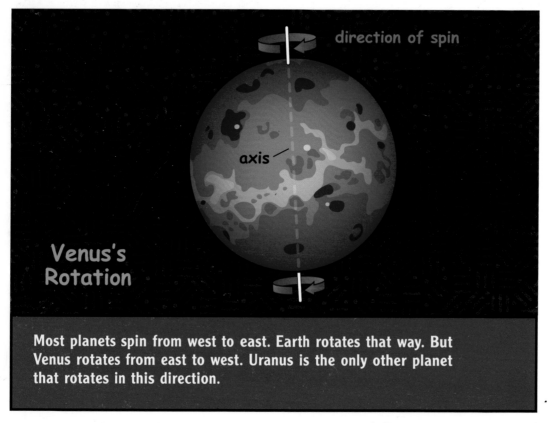

direction of spin

axis

Venus's
Rotation

Most planets spin from west to east. Earth rotates that way. But Venus rotates from east to west. Uranus is the only other planet that rotates in this direction.

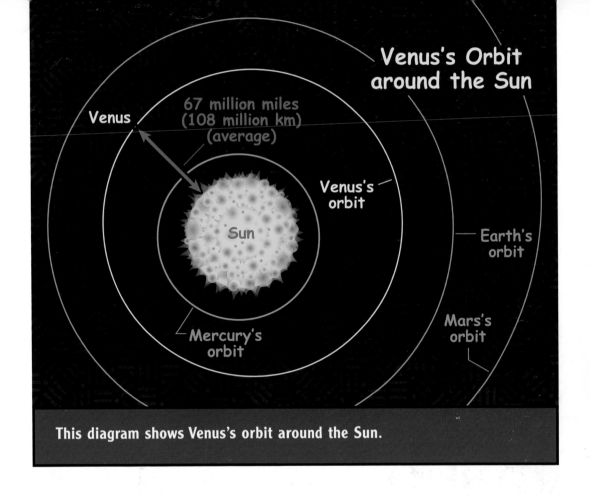

Venus's Orbit around the Sun

Venus

67 million miles
(108 million km)
(average)

Sun

Venus's orbit

Earth's orbit

Mars's orbit

Mercury's orbit

This diagram shows Venus's orbit around the Sun.

Each planet also follows its own path around the Sun. This oval-shaped path is called an orbit. One complete orbit is a year on a planet.

Venus's orbit is smaller than Earth's. So it orbits the Sun more quickly. Venus takes 225 Earth days to orbit the Sun. So Venus's year is shorter than its day!

Astronomers used special equipment to photograph Venus as it passed between Earth and the Sun. The photo shows Venus's shadowed side as a black dot.

Sometimes Venus is between Earth and the Sun. Then we can't see Venus at all. The sunny side of Venus faces away from us.

We also can't see Venus when it's on the other side of the Sun. The bright Sun hides the much smaller planet.

When we can see Venus from Earth, it looks crescent shaped. The Sun lights up one side of the planet. The other side is in shadow. The side that faces us is partly lit by sunlight and partly in shadow.

A telescope (TEH-luh-skohp) lets us see the crescent shape. Telescopes make faraway objects look bigger and closer.

We can't see Venus's crescent shape with our eyes. It is too far away. This picture was taken through a telescope.

Clouds of steam and poisonous gas rise from a hole in Earth's surface. What gases are in Venus's air?

CHAPTER 3

AROUND VENUS

Venus is surrounded with clouds. They hide its surface. Earth's clouds are made of water. But Venus's clouds are mostly made of sulfuric acid. Sulfuric acid is a strong chemical. It can dissolve rock and eat through metal.

Venus's clouds are part of its atmosphere (AT-muhs-feer). The atmosphere is a layer of gases that surrounds a planet. We call Earth's atmosphere air. We breathe oxygen in the air to live.

We couldn't breathe on Venus. Venus's atmosphere has almost no oxygen. It is mostly carbon dioxide (CAR-buhn dy-OX-eyed).

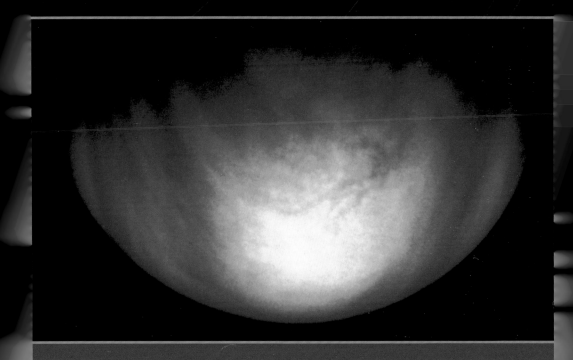

Clouds hide Venus's surface from view. In this picture, the Sun's light shines on cloud formations in Venus's thick atmosphere.

Carbon dioxide in the planet's atmosphere keeps heat from escaping into space. Carbon dioxide acts like glass in a greenhouse. It holds in the Sun's heat. We call this the greenhouse effect. This explains why Venus is so hot.

Tropical plants grow inside a warm greenhouse. Outside, the weather is freezing cold. Carbon dioxide in Venus's atmosphere acts like the greenhouse ceiling. It lets heat and light into the planet's atmosphere. Then it keeps heat from escaping.

Scientists think that Venus's dense, cloudy atmosphere might create the right conditions for lightning. An artist created this picture of lightning over Venus's mountains.

Venus's atmosphere is very dense. Its gases are packed together tightly. They weigh 90 times as much as our air. The gases press down on the planet's surface. They push with crushing force.

This Russian spacecraft, named *Venera 3*, was supposed to study Venus. But it broke apart and crashed on the planet's surface.

Venus's atmosphere makes it hard to explore the planet with spacecraft. These machines travel from Earth into space. They take pictures and send back information.

Spacecraft have landed on Venus. When they land, the dense gases in Venus's atmosphere press down on them. This pressing force can break spacecraft apart. Some spacecraft have been broken up before they landed. Others lasted just a few minutes.

There is little wind at the planet's surface. But high above, the winds are strong. They blow about 220 miles (350 km) per hour. That is faster than the strongest hurricane on Earth.

ABOVE: An astronomer took these pictures of Venus at different points in its orbit. They show clouds moving across the planet's surface. **RIGHT:** Computer-enhanced pictures show clouds spinning high above Venus's south pole.

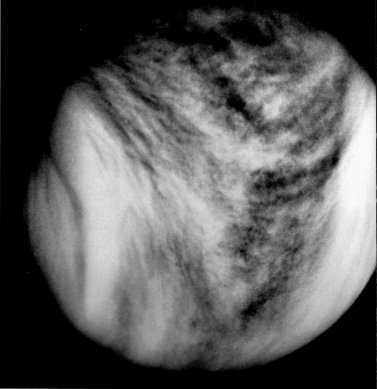

The *Pioneer Venus Orbiter* took this picture of Venus in 1979. Scientists used these pictures to make maps of Venus. What does Venus's surface look like?

CHAPTER 4

ON VENUS

Many spacecraft have traveled around Venus. Some of them have orbited the planet. They used radar to get pictures of Venus. Radar uses radio waves to take pictures through clouds. With these pictures, scientists could see Venus's surface, so they made maps.

Spacecraft have also landed on Venus. The photos these spacecraft took showed that the surface is rocky. They have found mountains, canyons, and craters. Craters are deep, bowl-shaped dents on the surface. Scientists have named these features on Venus after goddesses or famous women.

The spacecraft *Venera 13* landed on Venus in 1982. It took this photo of the planet's rocky surface.

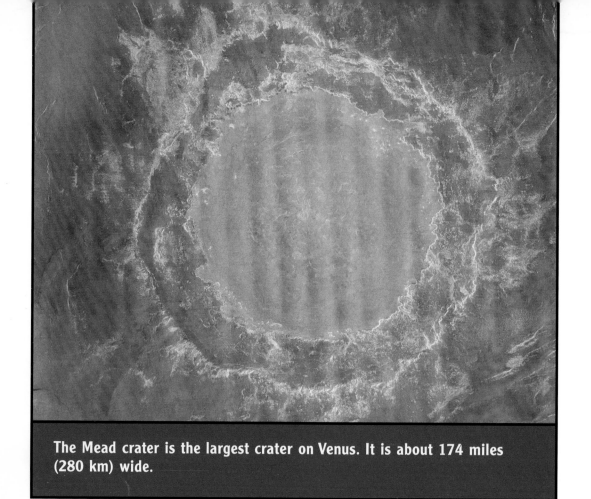

The Mead crater is the largest crater on Venus. It is about 174 miles (280 km) wide.

The largest crater on Venus is named for Margaret Mead. She was a famous U.S. scientist. Another crater is named Cleopatra for an ancient Egyptian queen. Another is named for Harriet Tubman. She fought against slavery in the United States.

Some of the mountains on Venus are very tall. Maxwell Montes is the highest. It rises 7 miles (11 km) above the surface. Mount Everest is the highest mountain on Earth. But Maxwell Montes is 1.5 miles (2.5 km) higher.

This mountain is named for James Clerk Maxwell, a British scientist. It's one of the only places on Venus named for a man.

Researchers used radar images to create this picture of Maxwell Montes (CENTER).

Many of the mountains on Venus are volcanoes. They pour out hot, melted rock called lava. Lava flows across the ground. It hardens into solid rock.

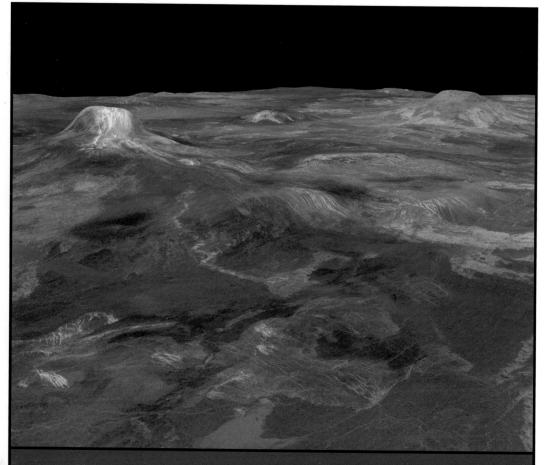

Lava formed the land around two of the volcanoes on Venus's surface. The volcano at top left is named Gula Mons, and the volcano at top right is Sif Mons. Astronomers used radar information to create this picture.

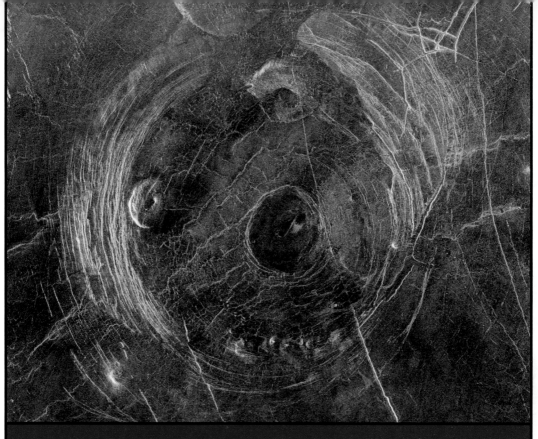

This photo shows the Aine Corona (CENTER). It is about 120 miles (200 km) wide. The corona is surrounded by cracks created when it sank.

Venus also has large, round regions where the ground has sunk. They are called coronas. They were probably formed when melted rock moved below the surface. The melted rock pushed the surface up. And when the hot rock flowed away, the surface sank.

A huge canyon cuts across part of Venus. This long, narrow channel is 4,588 miles (7,400 km) long. It's the longest channel on any planet in the solar system.

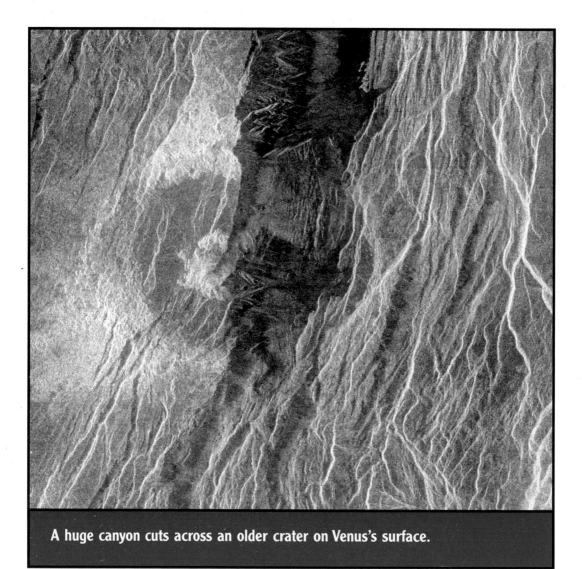

A huge canyon cuts across an older crater on Venus's surface.

An artist created this picture of Venus's largest canyon. Its walls are 3.7 miles (6 km) tall at their highest point.

The canyon is a mystery. How did it form? No one knows. On Earth, rivers carve out canyons. But Venus has no water. It's much too hot. Water would boil away. So a river didn't make the canyon. Could a river of lava have made it?

ABOVE: Cracks break up a flat stretch of Venus's surface. LEFT: The dark area of this photo is a flat plain. The brighter lines are a section of cracked and folded land.

Some parts of Venus are flat. In these places, the surface is cracked. The cracks form large rectangles that look like huge tiles.

The center of Venus is probably like Earth's center. It is probably made of metal. A rocky layer probably surrounds the center. But no one knows for sure.

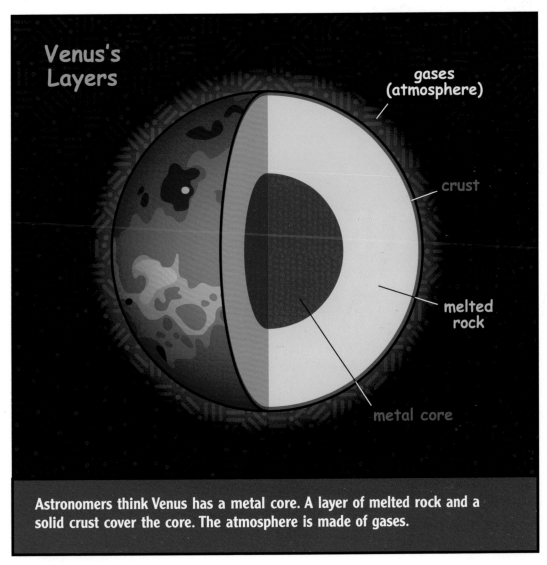

Venus's Layers

gases (atmosphere)

crust

melted rock

metal core

Astronomers think Venus has a metal core. A layer of melted rock and a solid crust cover the core. The atmosphere is made of gases.

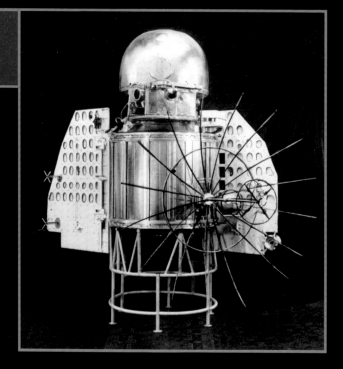

CHAPTER 5
VISITING VENUS

The first spacecraft to travel to Venus was *Venera 1*. It was launched in 1961. But scientists lost contact with it before it could send back information about Venus.

Mariner 2 was launched in 1962. It was the first spacecraft to study another planet. It flew past Venus. It took measurements and sent them to Earth.

Venera 4 was launched in 1967. It sent out a measuring instrument called a probe. It found that Venus's atmosphere was mostly made up of carbon dioxide. But the probe broke before it landed.

Venera 7 made it to Venus's surface in 1970. It was the first spacecraft to successfully land on another planet. It measured the temperature at the surface. But after 23 minutes, it stopped working.

A Russian scientist prepares *Venera 4* for launch in 1967.

Mariner 10 was launched in 1974. It flew past Venus. It took 3,000 photographs. Later, it flew past Mercury.

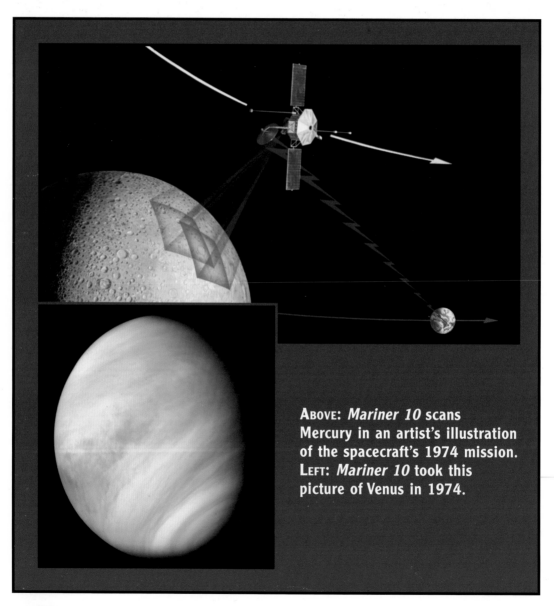

ABOVE: *Mariner 10* scans Mercury in an artist's illustration of the spacecraft's 1974 mission. **LEFT:** *Mariner 10* took this picture of Venus in 1974.

Researchers used radar images from *Magellan* to show the rocky surface of Venus. The reddish colors show the highest areas and the blue colors show the lowest areas of the surface.

Magellan was launched in 1989. *Magellan* circled Venus for four years. It used radar to map the surface. It measured Venus's gravity. Gravity is a force that pulls objects toward one another.

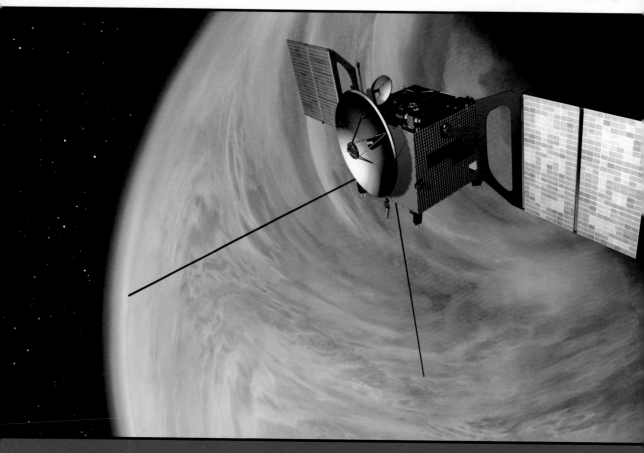

This illustration shows *Venus Express* in orbit around Venus in 2005.

Venus Express was launched in 2005. This spacecraft orbited Venus. It studied the atmosphere hidden below the clouds. It also measured wind speeds and studied the heat in the atmosphere.

Scientists are planning other missions to Venus. The next is called the *Venus Climate Orbiter "Planet-C."* It will study Venus's weather. It will look for lightning and active volcanoes. Scientists hope to launch it in 2010. They still have more to learn about Earth's twin.

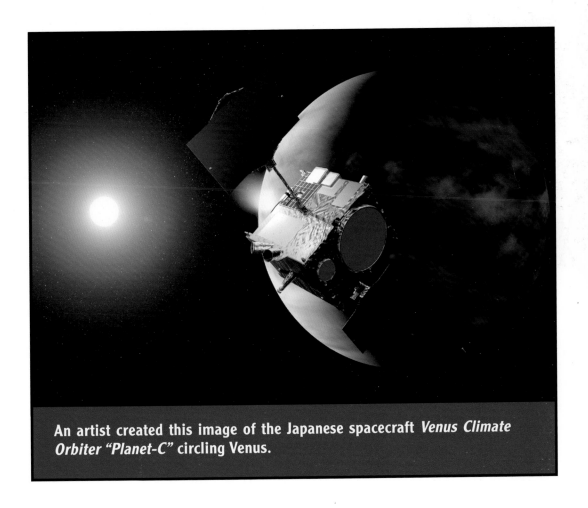

An artist created this image of the Japanese spacecraft *Venus Climate Orbiter "Planet-C"* circling Venus.

ON SHARING A BOOK

When you share a book with a child, you show that reading is important. To get the most out of the experience, read in a comfortable, quiet place. Turn off the television and limit other distractions, such as telephone calls. Be prepared to start slowly. Take turns reading parts of this book. Stop occasionally and discuss what you're reading. Talk about the photographs. If the child begins to lose interest, stop reading. When you pick up the book again, revisit the parts you have already read.

BE A VOCABULARY DETECTIVE

The word list on page 5 contains words that are important in understanding the topic of this book. Be word detectives and search for the words as you read the book together. Talk about what the words mean and how they are used in the sentence. Do any of these words have more than one meaning? You will find the words defined in a glossary on page 46.

WHAT ABOUT QUESTIONS?

Use questions to make sure the child understands the information in this book. Here are some suggestions:

What did this paragraph tell us? What does this picture show? What do you think we'll learn about next? Which planet is between Venus and the Sun? How is Venus's atmosphere different from Earth's? What can be found on the surface of Venus? What are the names of some of these places? What is your favorite part of the book? Why?

If the child has questions, don't hesitate to respond with questions of your own, such as What do *you* think? Why? What is it that you don't know? If the child can't remember certain facts, turn to the index.

INTRODUCING THE INDEX

The index helps readers find information without searching through the whole book. Turn to the index on page 48. Choose an entry such as *telescope* and ask the child to use the index to find out how telescopes help astronomers. Repeat with as many entries as you like. Ask the child to point out the differences between an index and a glossary. (The index helps readers find information, while the glossary tells readers what words mean.)

LEARN MORE ABOUT
VENUS

BOOKS

Loewen, Nancy. *Brightest in the Sky: The Planet Venus*. Mankato, MN: Picture Window Books, 2008. Explore Venus in this brightly illustrated book.

Miller, Ron. *Venus*. Minneapolis: Twenty-First Century Books, 2002. Learn more about Earth's nearest neighbor in space, Venus.

Peddicord, Jane Ann. *Night Wonders*. Watertown, MA: Charlesbridge, 2005. Take a journey through space with this poetic book.

Ride, Sally, and Tam O'Shaughnessy. *Exploring Our Solar System*. New York: Crown, 2003. An astronaut gives a tour of the planets.

WEBSITES

European Space Agency: Venus Express Mission
http://www.esa.int/esaMI/Venus_Express
Get information about the *Venus Express* mission.

Jet Propulsion Laboratory: Magellan Mission to Venus
http://www2.jpl.nasa.gov/magellan
Learn about the *Magellan* mission to Venus at this NASA site.

NASA SpacePlace
http://spaceplace.nasa.gov/en/kids
NASA's website for kids has activities, quizzes, and games about outer space.

The Nine Planets
http://kids.nineplanets.org/venus.htm
Read about Venus and the other planets in the solar system on this website.

Solar System Exploration
http://solarsystem.nasa.gov/kids
Get more information about all the objects in the solar system from this NASA site.

GLOSSARY

asteroids (A-stur-oydz): rocky bodies, much smaller than a planet, that exist in outer space

astronomer (uh-STRAH-nuh-muhr): a scientist who studies outer space

atmosphere (AT-muhs-feer): the layer of gases that surrounds a planet

axis (AK-sihs): an imaginary line that goes through a planet from top to bottom. A planet spins on its axis.

carbon dioxide (CAR-buhn dy-OX-eyed): a clear, colorless gas. Most of Venus's atmosphere is carbon dioxide.

coronas: large, round areas on the surface of Venus

day: the time a planet takes to spin around once

gravity: a force that pulls objects toward one another

orbit: the oval-shaped path a planet, moon, or other object travels in space

rotate (ROH-tayt): to spin around like a top

solar system: a group of planets and other objects that travel around the Sun

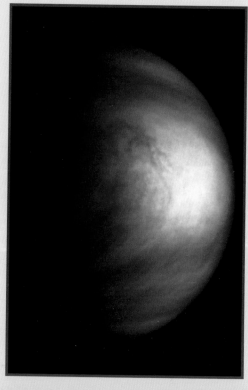

spacecraft: machines that travel from Earth to outer space

telescope (TEH-luh-skohp): an instrument that makes faraway objects look bigger and closer

volcanoes: mountains formed by hot melted rock, called lava, that hardens into rock

year: the time a planet takes to travel its path around the Sun

INDEX

Pages listed in **bold** type refer to photographs.